TEC

21st Century Skills Library

HEALTH AT RISK

BULIMIA

Gail B. Stewart

Cherry Lake Publishing
Ann Arbor, Michigan

Published in the United States of America by Cherry Lake Publishing
Ann Arbor, Michigan
www.cherrylakepublishing.com

Content Advisor: Carolyn Walker, RN, PhD, Professor, School of Nursing, San Diego
State University, San Diego, California

Photo Credits: Cover and page 1, © Oliver Hoffman/Shutterstock; page 4, © Simone
ver der Berg/Shutterstock; page 6, © SW Productions/Alamy; page 7, © Bubbles
Photolibrary/David Robinson/Alamy; page 9, © Bubbles Photolibrary/Angela
Hampton/Alamy; page 12, AP Images/Jake Schoellkopf; page 14, © David J. Green,
Lifestyle/Alamy; page 17, © Max Von Oxtail/Alamy; page 18, © Angela Hampton/Alamy;
page 19, AP Images/Kansas City Star, Kelly Chin; page 21, Maury Aaseng; page 22,
© Rob Melnychuk/Alamy; page 24, AP Images/Kevor Djansezian; page 27, © Bubbles
Photolibrary/Chris Rout/Alamy; page 29, © Collection 6/Alamy

Library of Congress Cataloging-in-Publication Data
Stewart, Gail B. (Gail Barbara), 1949–
 Bulimia / Gail B. Stewart.
   p. cm.—(Health at risk)
 ISBN-13: 978-1-60279-282-1
 ISBN-10: 1-60279-282-8
 1. Bulimia—Juvenile literature. I. Title. II. Series.
 RC552.B84S74 2008
 616.85'263—dc22   2008017497

*Cherry Lake Publishing would like to acknowledge the work of
The Partnership for 21st Century Skills.
Please visit www.21stcenturyskills.org for more information.*

TABLE OF CONTENTS

CHAPTER ONE

THE ILLNESS THAT PEOPLE HIDE

Bulimia has nothing to do with real hunger. Bulimics overeat to the point of becoming ill, then throw up the food they binge on.

Bulimia is an eating disorder. The name "bulimia" comes from two Greek words that mean "ox-hunger." That's a good name, because people with bulimia sometimes eat like an ox. People with bulimia might eat an entire pizza and a tub of ice cream. Then they might eat a whole bag of chips or cookies. They eat and eat until their stomachs hurt. This kind of eating is called binging.

There is a second part of bulimia. After binging, people with bulimia make their body get rid of the food. They force themselves to vomit. Or they take drugs that cause diarrhea. That gets rid of the food before it can

Bulimics and anorexics have certain traits in common, including the notion that they have very little control over their lives. They use food to feel in control.

make them gain weight. This part of bulimia is called purging.

Experts say that anywhere from 2 million to 6 million people suffer from bulimia

A young woman purges after having binged.

sometime in their lives. Bulimia can affect people of any age, race, or sex. But some groups tend to be at higher risk. For example, athletes tend to have a higher risk of bulimia. And it's known that bulimia affects at least four times as many girls as boys.

But experts do not know for sure how many people are bulimic because bulimia is a disease that people hide.

Most of the time, around other people, bulimics eat normally. They wait until no one can see them to binge and purge. So they can go for a long time before anyone suspects they have bulimia.

This is a problem because bulimia is a dangerous disease. Repeated vomiting can cause serious harm. It causes bleeding in the stomach and throat. It rots the teeth and turns them brown. It can affect the normal rhythm of the heart, which can lead to a heart attack and sudden death. Sadly, between 10 and 20 percent of people who have bulimia will eventually die from the disease unless they receive medical help.

CHAPTER TWO

How Do You Get Bulimia?

*Bulimia often starts during the teen years as the pressures
of school, friends, and home become most intense.*

Like other eating disorders, bulimia occurs for many reasons. Sometimes it starts when a person is unhappy or stressed and turns to food for comfort. For instance, the stress of moving away from home can lead to unhealthy eating habits. Maddie is a 24-year-old woman from Ottawa, Canada, who went away to college at age 18. Maddie was homesick. It was hard for her to make friends. She used food to help her deal with her loneliness. "I put on twenty pounds, pretty fast," she says. "Instead of dieting, I'd just make myself throw up. A lot of girls in my dorm did it to keep the weight off."

3 1833 05514 2175

Sometimes bulimia starts when a person is on a diet. That's what happened to Corrie, a 17-year-old from La Grange, Illinois. Corrie gave up foods she loved, like french fries and desserts. She lost a few pounds. But one day she felt really hungry. "I cheated," she admits. "I went through McDonald's and got a Big Mac, fries, and a chocolate shake. I ate really fast, and I felt sick. I threw up a few minutes later. After that, I'd cheat a few times a week, and throw up on purpose."

Boys get bulimia, too. The risk of bulimia is higher for boys that play sports with weight limits. For instance, wrestlers are put into classes according to their weight. Every wrestler must weigh in before a match. If he is too heavy, he can't compete. Tony was a wrestler on his Iowa high school team. He developed bulimia in his junior year. "I was in the 160-pound class," he says. "But I'd get nervous the week before a big meet. I eat when I'm

Jeff Everts, 43, plays with his dog Cheyenne in the backyard of his home. Everts is recovering from anorexia and bulimia, eating disorders among men that are getting worse, according to researchers.

nervous. A guy on the team told me he had the same problem. He told me to take laxatives after I ate. The food doesn't stay in you, so you don't gain weight. It was easy. But I didn't know how much damage it would do to my body. The laxatives gave me severe cramps. Even after I stopped using them, I had terrible stomachaches."

People with bulimia may not be able to hide their disorder. Doctors say these may be signs that someone you know has bulimia:
- Seems depressed.
- Visits the bathroom right after eating.
- Eats a great deal, but does not seem to gain weight.
- Seems driven to exercise.
- Seems too concerned about weight.
- Uses laxatives on a regular basis.

CHAPTER THREE

A Day in the Life

Like many addictive behaviors, a bulimic's habit can quickly become uncontrollable. Getting the support of a caring adult is necessary to help the bulimic quit.

Bulimia can take over a person's life. Corrie found that out the hard way. At first, she found herself binging and purging three times a week. Soon, it was every day, sometimes two or three times a day. "I bought pounder bags of M&Ms," she says. "And chips and other junk food. I had stashes under my bed and in my closet. It was expensive. I stole money from my sister to buy more food. I felt like a drug addict."

People with bulimia don't want others to know their eating is out of control. Corrie says she only binged when no one else was home. She says at first it felt good to feel full. But the good feeling did not last long. Soon, she

People with bulimia work hard to keep their binging and purging a secret. Even so, a friend or family member may discover what's happening. Make a list of things that might signal that someone close to you has bulimia. What would you do if you noticed any of these signals in a friend? Why do you think it might be difficult to confront that friend?

felt ashamed for eating so much. "I would have died if someone saw me stuffing all that food in my mouth," Corrie says. "I would eat with two hands. It was like I was a starving animal. I kept eating when I wasn't even hungry. It was really disgusting."

It's harder to keep purging secret. It's difficult to vomit quietly. Some bulimics turn the shower on while they purge to drown out the sound. Or they go outside, where people won't see or hear them. "I did that," says Maddie. "I didn't want to throw up at home. Someone would hear. So I'd go behind our garage. If you have bulimia, you learn to be really sneaky."

Bulimics suffer alone, carefully hiding their behavior from family and friends.

A young woman raids the refrigerator late at night. Bulimics are intensely secretive.

People with bulimia try to keep their disease secret, but the effects of bulimia can't be hidden. Friends and family may not notice the binging or purging. But sooner or later, everyone will notice that something is wrong.

CHAPTER FOUR

BODY DESTRUCTION

*Bulimics can destroy the enamel on their teeth and
cause chemical changes in their organs.*

Learning & Innovation Skills

Many eating disorder experts worry that the Internet can play a role in developing bulimia. Some people who suffer from anorexia or bulimia have Web sites that praise the disorders. They post updates about their weight loss and pictures of super-skinny models. They give tips on how to starve yourself and how to keep the disorders secret from other people. For instance, one pro-mia (short for pro-bulimia) site recommended chewing dozens of pieces of sugar-free gum as a laxative, to help someone purge. Many people believe these sites are dangerous because they make kids think that bulimia is OK. They feel the sites should be shut down. Others feel that even if the message is wrong, people with eating disorders have a right to free speech. What is your opinion? Why do you feel this way?

Some of the effects of bulimia are easy to see. Maddie soon noticed the bruises on her hands. When she forced herself to vomit, she stuck her fingers down her throat. When she gagged, her fingers would scrape against her teeth. "I had big scratches on my fingers that turned into bruises," she says. "And they never had time to heal. I was purging several times a week."

Frequent vomiting harms other parts of the body. It causes swelling around the jaw and neck and makes the face look puffy. Also, when someone throws up again and again over long periods of time, stomach

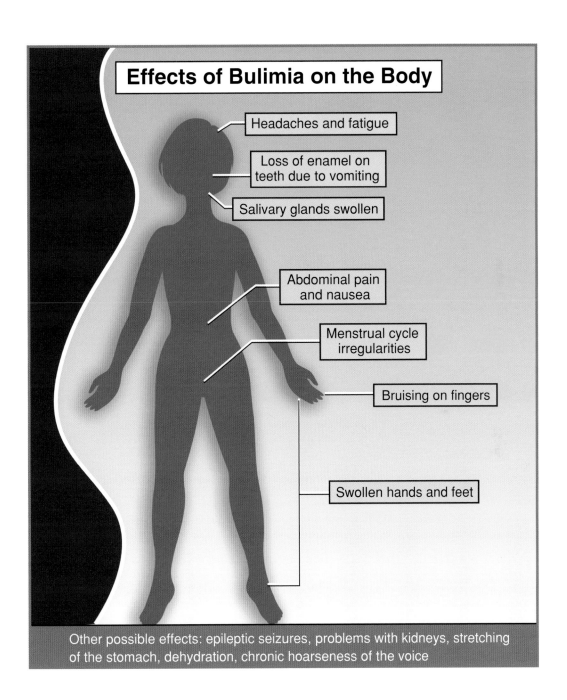

Effects of Bulimia on the Body

Headaches and fatigue

Loss of enamel on teeth due to vomiting

Salivary glands swollen

Abdominal pain and nausea

Menstrual cycle irregularities

Bruising on fingers

Swollen hands and feet

Other possible effects: epileptic seizures, problems with kidneys, stretching of the stomach, dehydration, chronic hoarseness of the voice

A bulimic can become overwhelmed by the behavior, and ignore all of the dangerous health effects that the disease produces.

acid comes up with the food. That acid burns the skin of the esophagus, the tube that connects the throat to the stomach. Sometimes the esophagus tears and bleeds when a person vomits. This is extremely painful.

Stomach acid can also ruin teeth. People with bulimia vomit so often that this acid wears away the enamel of their teeth. Enamel protects the teeth. Without it, the front teeth can split and cavities form easily. The acid also turns bulimics' teeth brown, especially the front teeth. It makes their breath smell terrible, too.

Other effects are far more dangerous. Frequent vomiting can tear the stomach lining, causing life-threatening problems. Purging also destroys the balance of chemicals in the body. Chemical imbalance can damage the kidneys. It can upset the normal rhythm of the heartbeat and cause heart attacks.

Bulimia can affect the brain, too. A chemical imbalance can make it hard to think clearly. It can make a person feel even more depressed and anxious. In this state, people with bulimia might not to understand the damage they are doing to themselves. "It gets worse and worse," says Corrie. "And if you don't get help, you could die."

21st Century Content

Some people with bulimia use excessive exercise as a way of purging. Sonya, a college student, had trouble her freshman year. She tried to diet, but didn't have enough willpower to stick to it. "I hate throwing up, and I was afraid of laxatives. I didn't want to have diarrhea all the time. So I started exercising—a lot. I've always been athletic, but I went nuts. I would eat, like maybe a half a pizza. Then I'd run on the treadmill in the workout room. I'd run ten miles a day. Sometimes I'd set my alarm and run at night, too. I just couldn't stop—it was like I was addicted."

CHAPTER FIVE

FIGHTING BACK

Finalist Katharine McPhee performs during the final show of American Idol in 2006. McPhee struggled with bulimia for five years.

Many people who have bulimia deny they have a problem. They try to keep their binging and purging secret. They don't want other people interfering. But keeping that secret is very dangerous. Sometimes, it's hard to admit they need help even after the secret gets out. That's what happened to Maddie. Her brother noticed she disappeared after meals. One night after dinner, he followed her. He saw her vomiting outside and told their parents.

"I was mad at first," says Maddie. "At first I told them it was just a one-time thing. But then I knew I had to tell the truth. And they helped me. They got me into a treatment program for people with eating disorders."

The first step of treatment is to repair damage to the body. This could include dental work. Some sufferers need medical treatment for a damaged stomach or esophagus. Some need medicine to bring chemical levels back to normal.

The second step in recovery is to stop the cycle of binging and purging. Stopping such harmful behavior can be very hard to do. People with bulimia might need to spend time in a place where staffers can monitor their actions. Sometimes that place is a hospital ward for people with eating disorders. In some communities, there are special clinics that treat eating disorders.

Hospitals and eating disorder clinics work roughly the same way. The staff keeps track of everything the bulimia patient eats. They make sure he or she doesn't purge after eating. "You get used to a staffer coming into the bathroom with you," says Corrie. "It feels weird

Severe bulimics may need inpatient treatment in a clinic or hospital to change the behavior.

at first. I didn't like it. But otherwise, I know I'd have made myself throw up. I wouldn't have gotten better."

The third part of recovery from bulimia is therapy. That means learning why binging and purging started in the first place. Through therapy, people work to solve problems so they don't become bulimic again. Some talk with a counselor alone. Some meet in groups. Sometimes family members get therapy too. Parents and siblings need to know the warning signs of bulimia. They learn how to help the bulimia patient get healthy and stay healthy. "I was in group therapy," says Maddie. "There were five other kids my age, and we talked about

Because eating must happen every day, a bulimic must constantly struggle to change the behavior.

problems we'd had. We learned what things caused us to start binging and purgeing."

Maddie says she's getting better every day. "Sometimes I still think about purging. But I haven't done it in two years. And I feel so much better. I hope no one else has to go through this."

GLOSSARY

anorexia (an uh REX ee uh) an eating disorder that causes people to starve themselves, usually resulting in weight 15 percent or more below normal

binging (BIN jing) eating large amounts of food in a very short time

bulimic suffering from bulimia

cycle (SI kuhl) a series of events that happens again and again

eating disorder an unhealthy, extreme concern with food, body image, and dieting

enamel (ee NAM uhl) the outer protective layer of teeth

esophagus (ee SOF uh guss) the tube connecting the throat and stomach

laxatives (LAKS uh tivz) substances that speed up bowel movements

monitor (MON uh turr) watch over, keep track of

purging (PER jing) getting rid of food after eating by vomiting or other methods

staffers paid workers

therapy (THARE uh pee) counseling or treatment to cure physical or psychological problems

FOR MORE INFORMATION

Books

Lawton, Sandra Augustyn, ed. *Eating Disorder Information for Teens: Health Tips About Anorexia, Bulimia, Binge Eating, and Other Eating Disorders.* Detroit: Omnigraphics, 2005.

Smith, Grainne. *Anorexia and Bulimia in the Family: One Parent's Practical Guide to Recovery.* West Sussex, England: John Wiley & Sons, 2004.

Watson, Stephanie. *Anorexia.* New York: Rosen, 2007.

Web Sites

American Anorexia Bulimia Association (AABA)
www.aabainc.org/home.html
Information about support groups for people fighting bulimia, referral networks, and eating disorder educational materials.

The Federal Government Source for Women's Health Information
www.4women.gov/faq/Easyread/bulnervosa-etr.htm
Easy-to-understand answers to common questions about bulimia, information about therapy and the physical effects of bulimia.

Mama's Health.com
www.mamashealth.com/eat
Easy-to-understand information about anorexia and bulimia. The site also offers first-person accounts from survivors of eating disorders and explains available therapies.

Mirror-Mirror, Eating Disorders Shared Awareness (EDSA) Canada
www.mirror-mirror.org/eatdis.htm
Bulimia information includes recommended reading and directories of national organizations and treatment centers all over Canada.

INDEX

ABOUT THE AUTHOR

Gail B. Stewart is the author of more than 220 books for children and young adults. She is the mother of three sons, and lives in Minneapolis, Minnesota.